OTTAWA
OVER TIME

B. Whitefield / NATIONAL ARCHIVES OF CANADA / C-000601

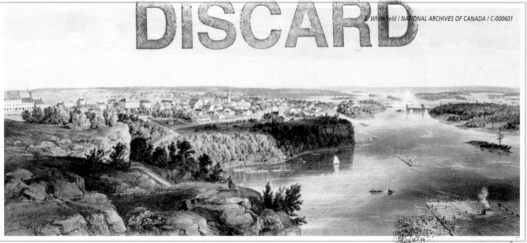

MAGIC LIGHT PUBLISHING

No other nation's state edifices can boast a more spectacular site than these high bluffs occupied by Canada's neo-gothic Parliament Buildings. Only three decades ago, this scene was also one of vibrant industry - complete with log booms, tugs and the ever present sounds and smells of a thriving lumber town. Now the sunny shores of Entrance Bay are accessed by cyclists and tourists, who find their way down to the water's edge via the Rideau Canal locks or the pathways that follow the river.

Known as the second coldest national capital in the world, Ottawa can be a harsh and forbidding place when the fierce winds of winter come. Now the waters of Entrance Bay are frozen two feet thick and both the Rideau Canal locks and Chateau Laurier Hotel are lost from sight in the driving snow. The freshly fallen snow obscures the embankment where the river ends and the grounds of the Canadian Museum of Civilization begin.

IN THE BEGINNING

The interior of the sleeping North American continent was most easily reached in the 17th century by an ancient aboriginal "Highway" - the Ottawa River, the Mighty Kitchisppi, river of the Algonquin. The river irresistibly beckoned European explorers, fur traders and missionaries along its 1280 kilometres (800 miles) from the St. Lawrence River, along the Ottawa and then via Lake Huron to the abundance of the Mississippi Valley, the vast plains of the north west and the rich potential of the Arctic and Pacific oceans.

NATIONAL ARCHIVES OF CANADA / C-2774

Francis Anne Hopkins / NATIONAL ARCHIVES OF CANADA / C-002773

The Voyageurs, who opened up the vast lands to the north and west, brought their furs down the Ottawa to Montreal, to be shipped to fashionable Europeans. While they prided themselves in their excellent handling of the massive "canôts du nord", they didn't think twice about putting ashore to portage around the Chaudiére. Sleeping under their large, birch bark canoes to protect themselves from the elements, these fur traders and their native counterparts traditionally made use of camp sites at the present day location of the Museum of Civilization and at Chaudiére Falls.

Statue of French explorer Samuel de Champlain atop Nepean Point, overlooking the Ottawa River behind the National Gallery of Canada.

In the early part of the 19th century, Chaudiére Falls (named after the French word for cauldron - a reference to the steamy mists that boiled off the raging water in winter) was still a wild and untamed torrent.

The "boiling cauldron" of Ottawa's thundering Chaudiére Falls was an enforced rest stop along the way. And it never failed to impress all who came upon it. The following is how Champlain first described it in 1613.

"A league thence we passed a rapid which is half a league wide and has a descent of six or seven fathoms (36 or 42 feet). Here are many small islands which are nothing more than rough, steep rocks, covered with poor, scrubby wood. At one place the water falls with such force upon a rock that with the lapse of time it has hollowed out a wide, deep basin. Herein the water whirls around to such an extent, and in the middle sends up such big swirls, that the Indians call it Asticou, which means 'boiler'. This waterfall makes such a noise in this basin that it can be heard for more than two leagues away."

View of Chaudiére Falls looking north toward Hull in 1867, the year of Canadian Confederation.

Contemporary aerial view of the once mighty Chaudiére Falls, now subdued by hydro electric dams.

Contemporary aerial view of Chaudiére Falls area showing E.B. Eddy complex. Government building complex at top right of photo occupies site of the original Philemon Wright townsite begun in March of 1800.

Wright's growing commerce brought him into partnerships with voyageurs and lumbermen. Here he is depicted completing an upstream portage in 1818 with a group of rugged voyageurs, as raftsmen take a faster but more dangerous route downstream through a stretch of white water.

WRIGHTSTOWN, CRADLE FOR CANADA'S CAPITAL

In the Spring of 1800, the world's attention was focused on Napoleon, as he consolidated his conquest of Italy. That same spring, far from the eye of the world, a visionary American from Boston had begun clearing land to build a settlement he would call Wrightstown, beside the Chaudiére Falls, where the city of Hull, Quebec now stands. Philemon Wright's original group would, 200 years later, have grown to a National Capital with a population of some 750,000 people.

Philemon Wright saw potential for a mill here at the edge of the tumbling water. And it was a going concern in this 1823 painting, employing many of the men who came north with him from Boston. Hard work made for a thirsty man and Wright made back some of the wages he paid out at his tavern right next to the mill.

In the photo above, one of J.R. Booth's rafts floats down river on the way to Québec City. The raftsmen were employed to steer the large rafts made of smaller cribs down river. When they reached the next stretch of white water, they were broken down into smaller crib units, sent over the rough water and then reassembled downstream. The raftsmen lived on the rafts, cooking their meals on a fire set upon a sand floor. Here we see them relaxing after a meal.

While it was Wright who pioneered the Ottawa Valley lumber trade, Ezra Buttler Eddy and John Rudolphus Booth picked up the torch and created vast business empires for themselves and the thriving community that grew up around them. They were the first of what would become known as 'lumber barons'.

J.R. Booth posing beside a flatcar loaded with his giant, square timbers.   *E.B. Eddy posing with his family in all their baronial splendor.*

THE RIDEAU CANAL

Following the War of 1812 between Canada and the United States, British military planners were desperate to establish a secure water route from Montreal to Kingston on Lake Ontario - this to avoid the danger of American guns along the south shore of the St. Lawrence River. Their solution was to build a canal from the point where the Rideau River entered the Ottawa and it was this decision that would set the stage for the creation of the city of Ottawa. Construction began on the 200 kilometre (120 miles) waterway under the supervision of Colonel John By, a British Army engineer, in 1826. The community of Bytown (later Ottawa) took root and flourished as the canal builders worked on this water highway.

Across the river from Philemon Wright's new town, engineers of the British Army begin construction of the locks that would enable watercraft to ascend from Entrance Bay to the Rideau Canal. Colonel John By (right) can be seen supervising army sappers as they labour to finish the lower lock. Behind, on the surface of the bay, we see two large rafts being maneuvered by the lumbermen on their way to mills downstream.

For many years, the locks at Entrance Bay were used only by commercial and military vessels. Nowadays they are employed only by pleasure craft making the climb or descent between the Ottawa River and the beautiful Rideau Waterway system, which ends 200 kilometres (120 miles) away at the Lake Ontario city of Kingston. These three views show a time lapse, as four pleasure boats are raised to the level of the last lock before entering the canal. The process of transiting the locks from the Ottawa River to the Rideau Canal eighty feet above, takes about two hours.

The Chateau Laurier Hotel, locks at Entrance Bay and Parliament Hill as seen from the spectacular pedestrian walkway of the Alexandra Bridge.

(Left) Observation Deck overlooking Entrance Bay, located at the Ottawa end of the Alexandra Bridge. The contemporary images on these pages were taken from here and if you do not spend a few minutes on this lookout during your visit to the National Capital, you are missing one of the truly spectacular vistas this city - and this country - has to offer.

(Inset above) Construction is just beginning on the Alexandra Bridge in March of 1898, when this photo was taken. The open air in the foreground is where, 100 years later, the lovely observation deck (at left) would be added to the bridge.

(Right) Fitzgibbon's Landing and locks as they appeared in 1842.

(Far right) Entrance Bay locks as they appear today. A sloop used for teaching youth about sailing tallships, steps her masts in readiness for an adventure on the spectacular Rideau Canal.

W.H. Bartlet / CITY OF OTTAWA ARCHIVES / CA-2690

Rideau Canal with Ottawa Congress Center and Westin Hotel in the background.

At sunrise, a lone sculler from the Bytown Boat Club rows past the opening to Patterson Creek, one of two inlets which lead into the upscale community known as the Glebe.

Tour boats, like the Ottawa Queen, now ply the Rideau Canal from Union Station to Dow's Lake. The wide tour boats are specially designed to navigate the low clearance of the hydraulically lifted Pretoria Bridge.

Winter or summer, the terminus of the Rideau Canal, with its spectacular environs, is one of the most photographed and painted spots in all of Ottawa. Pleasure boats of all descriptions tie up along its walls and, on a perfect summer evening the setting sun silhouettes the neo-gothic spires of Parliament and bathes the surface of By's canal with a golden light.

CANADIAN TULIP FESTIVAL

When Holland was invaded by the Nazis in 1940, Crown Princess Juliana found shelter for herself and her two daughters, Beatrix and Irene, in Ottawa. On returning home at war's end, a grateful Juliana sent 20,000 tulip bulbs to the city, "for services rendered in time of need," and every year since then many more thousands of bulbs have followed, giving rise to the Canadian Tulip Festival the largest tulip festival in the world.

For a brief ten days in the warm sunlight of early May, the Capital seems blanketed in fabulous colour. Ottawans join visitors from all corners of the world who come to enjoy Princess Juliana's gift, to take a picture amidst the blooms and to stroll through the endless sea of colour. From a tradition born of tragedy over fifty years ago, the tulip has become, like the Peace Tower and the Guardsman, an icon of Canada's Capital.

The Canadian Tulip Festival is scheduled to coincide with the blooming of the tulips, but after a particularly mild winter, the tulips can be out and gone before the ribbon is cut. Such are the risks of holding an outdoor festival, but that does not deter organizers. When the gates open and the music kicks in, Ottawans come out to work out the stiffness of the long winter months.

SPRING

The rigors of a typical Ottawa winter are quickly forgotten amidst the splendor of a sea of tulips that blankets the city in riotous colour. As if in competition with the tulips, fruit trees herald Spring's life-renewing call with their own spectacular display of blossoms. And when a carpet of daffodils is added to the tableau one would not be surprised to find Monet himself, risen from the grave to capture it all on canvas.

SNOWBIRDS

As Ottawa is the Nation's Capital, its citizens are blessed with many spectacles on or above Parliament Hill. Twice a year, during the National Capital Air Show and on Canada Day, the skies over Ottawa are the stage for a patriotic and heart-pounding flypast of the Canadian Air Force's 431 Air Demonstration Squadron, better known as The Snowbirds.

PARLIAMENT HILL

The Parliament Buildings and the lawns they surround, are icons of Canada's federal system and Ottawa's place in the Nation's history. On these lawns, we come together to celebrate, to mourn, to protest, to watch, to be heard and to share our heritage. This special open space has seen tradition and spectacle, peace and anger as well as frisbees and placards.

Ottawa is the capital city of a great northern country. We wear winter well. Here the ice-coated trees of Major's Hill Park sparkle in the bright midday sun. Across the locks from the park, and to the west, lies Parliament Hill and the snow-covered spires of the Centre Block and the Library. The true beauty of this architectural wonder is that it is breathtaking from every angle and from every vantage point. When architects were contemplating its design, they knew full well that the high site would afford views from all directions and they rose to the challenge.

The top photo shows progress of construction on the massive Centre Block of Parliament c. 1863. Tragically, fire destroyed this magnificent building in 1916. The present-day Centre Block (shown under construction c. 1919) was completed in 1927.

First lit in 1967, the Centennial Flame, surrounded by Coats of Arms of Canada's Provinces and Territories, holds its place of honour at the base of the walkway leading to the Peace Tower.

Like all things Canadian, the Centre Block and the Peace Tower come alive with winter. Each December, the National Capital Commission decks the trees and bushes around Parliament Hill with many thousands of coloured lights. Purples, reds, blues, greens and yellows of every description are worked together into a symphony of riotous colour. Crews work feverishly for weeks in sub-zero weather and, a fortnight before Christmas, thousands of Ottawans flock to the Hill for the throwing of the switch. At the appointed hour, the lights are switched on and the ooohs! and ahhhs! can be heard across the country. In an instant, the darkened ground of the Hill are transformed - much to the delight of children of all ages.

Storm clouds have cleared out from the west, enough to allow the setting sun to bathe the Alexandra Bridge in a sparkling golden hue, made all the more beautiful by the looming storm clouds behind. The Alexandra, or Interprovincial Bridge, today provides pedestrians with the most magnificent panoramas Ottawa has to offer.

The 300 foot gothic height of the Peace Tower is framed by the entrance portico of the East Block. The Parliament Buildings house the Senate, commons, Library and offices of Members of Parliament, Senators and their staffs.

For nearly a century, the silhouette of the Parliament Buildings and the swirling Ottawa River far below have made for the most spectacular of sunrises. Yet only a handful of Ottawans have ever witnessed these misty, marmalade skies, heard the cries of the wheeling seagulls or watched as the sun rose to warm the sandstone walls of Canada's greatest treasure. Every citizen should, at least once in a lifetime, set the alarm and take a stroll along the walkway behind the Canadian Museum of Civilization in Hull to take in the sight which remains privy only to intrepid photographers and insomniac joggers.

A setting sun, on yet another perfect evening, accentuates the details at the edge of the still waters. Viewed from the former Fitzgibbon's Landing below the bridge, the bullnose casements of the lower lock catch the same sun which highlights both tour boat and Parliamentary tower.

MAJOR'S HILL PARK

Aerial view of Parliament Hill looking west over Major's Hill Park, the Chateau Laurier Hotel, Confederation Square and the Entrance Bay Locks on the Rideau Canal.

Major's Hill, unlike most of Ottawa's parks, has been cherished green space since the very first days of our community. With a spectacular view up the river, Major's Hill went from estate to civic park without any interim development. Today it is a priceless piece of Canadian history. Visitors can visit the site of Colonel John By's original house and imagine what a lovely view he would have enjoyed as Bytown grew even larger under Canadian skies..

CHANGING THE GUARD

The Royal initials of E II R - Elizabeth II, Queen of England gleam on the polished mace of the Drum Major. In the dome we see the reflection of the Parliament buildings where, each day throughout the summer, impeccably turned out Guardsmen keep alive a tradition that has belonged to this city since the beginning of Confederation.

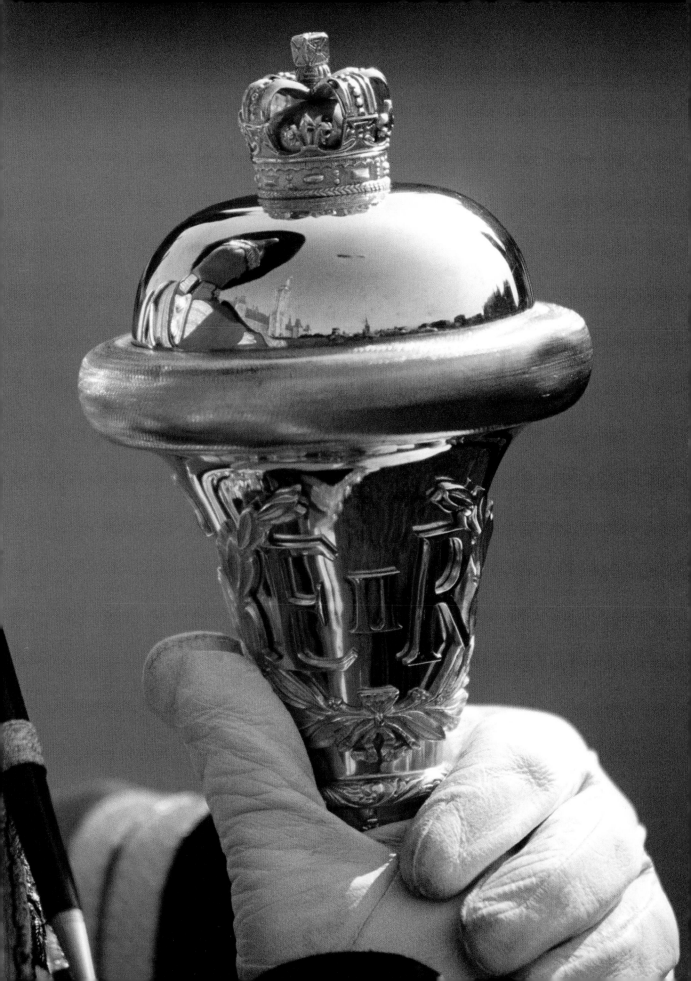

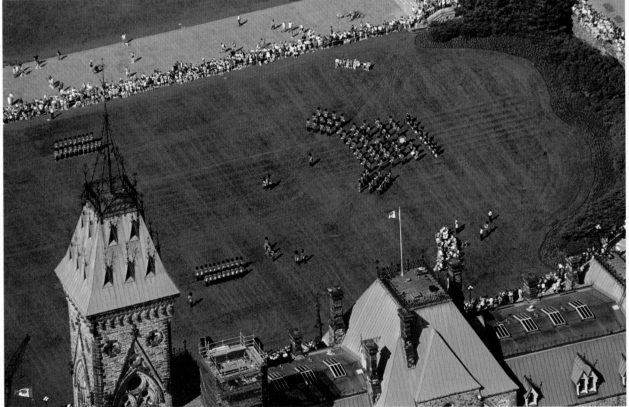

Shining brass, gold braid, scarlet tunic and immaculate leather. In an age of high-tech soldiering and electronic entertainment, the traditional uniforms, precise drill and stirring martial music of the Ceremonial Guard still raise goosebumps on the most jaded youth. Thousands of onlookers line the perimeter of the east lawn each day to view the spectacle. The 135 soldiers and bandsmen begin their daily march at the Cartier Square Drill Hall along the Rideau Canal. The rousing pipes and brass and the crunch of boots can be heard above the din of the city and many tourists rush from their hotels and adjoining streets to join them, as they move out for Parliament Hill.

The great sweeping vista of Confederation Square takes in the East Block of Parliament, the War Memorial and the Chateau Laurier Hotel. From high above the East Block, the Guardsmen below take on the dimensions of toy soldiers. The perfection of their close-order drill work is traced in the freshly mowed lawn in precise parallel lines. After the Changing the Guard Ceremony on Parliament Hill, the Ceremonial Band, with instruments silent, make their way south to Cartier Square Drill Hall.

NATIONAL ARCHIVES OF CANADA / PA-011864

RIDEAU HALL

Rideau Hall is not only an important part of Ottawa's heritage, but of Canada's as well. It is primarily the residence of the Governor General, the Queen's representative in Canada. At the outset, these Royal appointees were traditionally aristocrats from Great Britain, but since the days of Vincent Massey, they have been chosen from the ranks of accomplished and diplomatic Canadians. Rideau Hall is where all foreign ambassadors must present their Letters of Credence and where visiting heads of state are put up during their stay in the Nation's Capital. Grounds keepers take advantage, on some occasions, to have the dignitary plant a new tree on the lawn in front of the main entrance. A brief stroll through the trees will reveal plaques with the names of some of the world's most influential statesmen and figures - names like John F. Kennedy, Nelson Mandela, Dwight D. Eisenhower, Diana, Princess of Wales and Margaret Thatcher.

Originally constructed in 1838 by Thomas MacKay, a wealthy stonemason and contractor, the structure graced what was known then as "MacKay's Bush". The house, nicknamed "MacKay's Castle" was considered remote from the rest of Bytown, connected by little more than a path, but was chosen for its modern luxuries such as central heating and running water. Such was the state of the road that the first Governor General actually boarded a Royal Navy cutter at Governor's Bay on the river, below what is now the Prime Minister's Residence. He was then rowed the short distance to the Ottawa Locks, where a carriage awaited.

The name "Rideau Hall" is reported to have been suggested by MacKay's daughter Elizabeth in honour of the work he completed on the Rideau Canal and for his mills at Rideau Falls. Almost the entire structure of the original residence is hidden by a series of additions, which have been constructed since the initial purchase.

(Left) Their Royal Highnesses, the Duke and Duchess of Cornwall and York, at a reception at Rideau Hall, 1901.

In celebration of the 125th anniversary of the RCMP, Mounties dress in vintage Northwest Mounted Police uniforms to the delight of children and adults.

A piper leads three fresh Guardsmen of the Canadian Grenadier Guards out of the main gate of Rideau Hall to relieve the two who now stand to attention outside their posts. It is forbidden for sentries to talk to or acknowledge anyone, except in the line of duty. Just as in Great Britain, obnoxious tourists, attractive women and testy children will try to get a reaction from the sentries in many ways, but they must not, under any circumstances, react. The regal Main Gate of Rideau Hall is visible in the aerial view inset above.

An aerial view of the Rideau Hall grounds at the peak of fall colour shows us just how stunning this Canadian treasure is. At the bottom we see the open space of the traditional cricket pitch and at lower right, the gardens which are the site of much gracious hospitality. Virtually all of the large orange, red and yellow coloured trees along and below the main drive were planted by the world's greatest dignitaries. You will find there the names of kings and queens, dukes and duchesses, presidents and prime ministers, warriors and peacemakers. It is a special space open to all Canadians, but only a few short years ago, it was suggested that the grounds be closed to the public for security reasons. The outcry from Canadians who felt that it belonged to ordinary citizens, as much as to the world's elite, convinced officials to keep the gate open. This is truly our national home.

GATINEAU

For decades after the Great fire of 1900, Hull (renamed Gatineau in 2002) suffered from its effects. Homes that were destroyed by the fire were those of the working class families employed by the mills. Compensation was barely enough to close in a new home and for seventy years many of the houses in the downtown area remained virtually unfinished. Today, a revitalized downtown core with excellent restaurants, public parks and restored buildings makes the city of Hull a vibrant part of the Nation's Capital region.

From an aerial vantage point to the south of Chaudière Falls, (inset to left) we see the sweep of the river and four of the five bridges that join the two halves of the National Capital region. The complex dams and sluices of the still functioning E.B. Eddy mills mask the Chaudière Bridge and its series of spans.

A major part in the rebirth of the City of Hull was the decision to locate the Canadian Museum of Civilization to the old Eddy pulp mill site along the Ottawa River at Entrance Bay. This had the effect of anchoring positive development and bridging the river with the Nation's Capital. Not long after came the announcement that the government of Québec would build a world class casino at the old quarry near Leamy Lake. This spectacular and tasteful structure attracts tourists and citizens alike. In summer, the flooded quarry comes alive with towering fountains and a festival of fireworks that rivals Canada Day.

The busy pulp mill (above) on the site of today's Canadian Museum of Civilization dominated life and sight across from Parliament Hill for many years. In the 1950s, it was producing at its peak. The great mountains of pulpwood logs, put up for the winter, were gone by springtime, when the harvest started all over again.

The beautiful lines of the Canadian Museum of Civilization look more a part of the land than of the skyline. Since the creation of this world-class museum, the entire edge of the river has been revitalized. A landscaped path now enables people to completely circumnavigate Entrance Bay on foot or bicycle.

The Canadian Museum of Civilization, designed by renowned Canadian architect Douglas Cardinal, is the jewel in the crown of Hull's redevelopment. The evocative curvelinear forms and use of natural materials bring to mind the essence of the land, of history and of Canada. Cardinal's unique Métis perspective has created a design in harmony with the spirit of the place, for it was right here, only two centuries ago, that his forefathers, both native and French, made camp.

MUSEUMS

The Grand Hall of the Canadian Museum of Civilization (right) is an experience itself worth the price of admission. The centrepiece of this vast and spiritual space is a reconstruction of a Haida village. Throughout the museum, visitors can journey back through time and experience Canadian history first hand. Life-size set pieces let you actually walk down a street in Upper Canada at the turn of the century (below left) or visiting a fur traders cabin deep in the forest (below right)

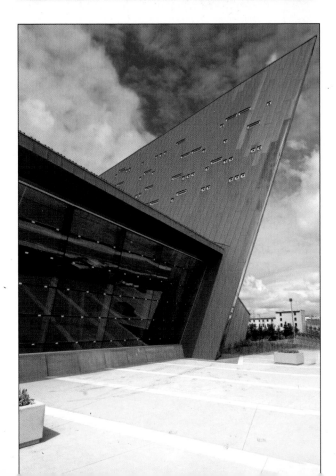

The Canadian War Museum moved into its spectacular new home in 2005. Based on the theme of Regeneration, it evokes not only the impact of war on the land but also nature's ability to regenerate itself after conflicts. From the grass-covered roof to the angled concrete walls that convey the instability of war, the building's architecture reflects the stories presented in the Museum. The Permanent Exhibition is divided into four chronological galleries. Each gallery highlights defining moments in Canada's military history and the ways in which past events have shaped the nation. More importantly, that history is told primarily through the stories of individuals.

Photo: Malak

Photo: Malak

Housing one of the greatest aircraft collections in the world, the National Aviation Museum is an ultra modern facility built on the site of one of Canada's historic military airfields. In years gone by, RCAF Station Rockcliffe reverberated to the snarling sounds of piston aircraft engines and the piercing shriek of the early jet age. Now the NAM welcomes visitors to it climate controlled interior where they can view the same aircraft which once haunted its runways as well as those from the long and rich history of Canadian civil aviation.

Early scheduled airline service in Canada is exemplified by this Lockheed 10A in the markings of Trans Canada Airlines, the predecessor of Air Canada.

(Below, left and reight) From the fire-scarred Apollo 7 command module to the fluffy contents of a chick incubator, the Museum of Science and Technology has something for everyone – especially kids.

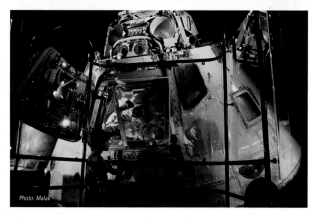

Photo: Malak

Photo: Malak

The Canadian Museum of Nature, a mammoth Victorian structure built at the start of the 20th century, now houses everything from dinosaur skeletons to spectacular dioramas showing Canada's native fauna and flora. The museum's flagship draw is its giant collection of dinosaur skeletons among which kids can camp out for the night.

(Below left) Canadian Galleries of the National Galery of Canada

AUTUMN

With the coming of fall, Ottawans are of two minds. We lament the passing of yet another warm and languid summer and start to feel the exhilaration that the increasingly colder mornings bring. Soon it will be winter, time for skating on the canal, skiing in the Gatineaus or tobogganing at the Central Experimental Farm. Getting out to enjoy the breathtaking colour of the fall leaves throughout the region is the perfect way to make the transition.

Golfers putt out at the 7th hole of the Larrimac Golf and Country Club. One of the Ottawa region's oldest courses, Larrimac, celebrating its 75th anniversary in 1999, offers nine of the most scenic holes in the Gatineaus.

The Prime Minister of Canada can take off a few hours from his or her busy schedule during the fall sitting of Parliament and enjoy the leaves from the official Prime Ministerial summer residence on private Harrington Lake (left).

Flying over the main quadrangle in front of Ottawa University's Tabaret Hall, we see that the fall colours have offered students yet another distraction.

Cyclists and runners alike can enjoy autumn and exercise at the same time. The pathways around the canal are smoothly paved and run in and out of the trees while remaining close to the canal all the way.

WINTER FUN

Downhill skiing has long been part of the fabric of growing up in Ottawa with it's many small, excellent ski slopes only a short drive away. And cross-country skiing has seen a phenomenal growth with outdoor and health enthusiasts over the past two decades. The best place for beginners and experts alike is the snow covered, track-set trails on the roadways of Gatineau Park. These scenic parkways, which cater to automobile and cycle traffic in the summer, are closed in the winter and given over to recreation. The increase in cross-country activity has spawned enormous interest in ski racing. Today, there are several ski races in the area, none more grueling than the 25-kilometer (15 mile) Keskinada Loppet.

It is often said that there are only two seasons in Ottawa - winter and four months of bad snowmobiling. For new Canadians, the first winter in Ottawa can be a bitter and depressing experience, especially if they come from sunnier climes. Some never get used to it, while others adjust. It's the next generation, one which was born into winter, that flourishes. Native-born citizens of Ottawa embrace the cold months, for they know there is much joy in its freeze. Others call it bitter; they call it crisp. Others see snow falling as a problem; they see snow falling as an opportunity for fun.

The biggest winter event in Ottawa is undoubtedly Winterlude, the celebration of our relationship with winter along the Rideau Canal. It is a time for even the most committed couch potato to lace up, to laugh and to feel the sun on the face and the ice underfoot. One thing strikes home when skating among the tens of thousands along the canal - everyone is smiling!

An afternoon at Winterlude can include a tour of the snow sculptures on Dow's Lake, a leisurely skate to Fifth Avenue for the obligatory Beavertail pastry or all the way to the National Arts Centre, if anyone is feeling really active. Along the way, skaters can enjoy outdoor figure skating demonstrations, food, and miles of the best natural ice in the world. NCC ice crews, well schooled in the science and art of ice making, prepare the canal afresh each night throughout the skating season.

During Winterlude, there are wonderful things for all ages to see and do, sled dog rides, snow and ice sculpting and the kids' favourite - the ice slides of Jacques Cartier Park.

Hillary Rodham Clinton, First Lady of the United States, chats with Pam and Grant Hooker after tasting their famous Beaver Tails.

KINGSMERE

In 1950, the more than 600-acre estate of the late Prime Minister William Lyon MacKenzie King was turned over to the federal government. The property, known as Kingsmere, was immediately incorporated into plans for development of the Gatineau Park region. At the heart of King's land was his summer residence, Moorside, which today functions as a teahouse and interpretive centre for the estate. Since King was unmarried and without heirs, he left this wonderful, silent woodland and its recuperative qualities for all Canadians to enjoy as he did during the most turbulent years of his leadership. He would be very happy to see that his wish has been carried out and that Canadians have come to consider it their own.

The ruins of Kingsmere, born from the creative mind of a great man, now stand year round as a tribute to his beliefs, his love of family and his personal history. In summer, thousands stop to see and understand. In winter, only intrepid naturalists and the animals of the forest come to share a moment with his spirit. King would probably like the winter visitors best of all.

Winter or summer, Kingsmere and Moorside have qualities that make them uniquely Canadian - natural, pristine, silent and elegant. In winter, cross-country skiers and snowshoers take advantage of the snowy setting to cast off the accumulated stresses of big city living.

King enjoyed meditation in the confines of his private ruins. Erected as a ruin, the structure was concocted with components from various meaningful sources - the old printing shop of his grandfather, the original Parliament Buildings which were destroyed by fire in 1916 and even the Parliament Buildings in London, England.

GATINEAU PARK

Gatineau Park is the National Capital's all-season playground. No time of year however, is more enjoyed than the peak of fall colour. From early morning until the sun sets at night, an endless parade of cars, cyclists and in-line skaters make the climb to the highest point on the park road system - the Champlain Lookout. The Lookout offers a spectacular view west along the Ottawa Valley and the very edge of the rolling Gatineau Hills. From here, one can see for twenty miles along the river that Champlain travelled so many years ago.

Throughout the entire region, the tumbling waters of our rivers and streams have provided the nucleus for development of our communities big and small - from E.B. Eddy's huge factories at Chaudière Falls to the small stone mill at Wakefield, Québec. Wakefield, a former mill and quarry town up the Gatineau River from Hull, is now one of the most popular tourist destinations in the region. Excellent restaurants, skiing, boutiques and bakeries make the scenic thirty-minute drive even more worthwhile.

The Wakefield Steam Train runs all summer long along the old rail bed on the west bank of the Gatineau River. Steam enthusiasts, tourists and local families take the twice-daily slow, rolling trip from Hull through Chelsea to Wakefield.

CASCADES

Waterways have played an important role in the history and development of Ottawa. The Rideau River, Ottawa River, Gatineau River and Rideau Canal functioned as the commercial arteries of the region for centuries and, in terms of tourism, still do.

Hog's Back Falls (above and right) is a wildly careening cacophony of crashing water, misting plumes, swirling eddies and multiple cascades.

Rideau Falls and Hog's Back Falls have remained somewhat the same since the days when voyageurs and native hunters were forced to portage around them. Both have their own distinct qualities. Rideau Falls (below) is a miniature Niagara, with two distinct curtains of Rideau River water slipping swiftly to their thundering deaths forty feet below, much to the delight of the passengers on the Paula D, an Ottawa River tour boat.

The Gatineau Hills are seamed with secret streams and waterfalls (right). A short hike from any road will bring you to a sun-dappled eddy or a rushing stream.

The photographs below show the same stretch of the Gatineau River near Ironside, Québec as it flows through four seasons from autumn's rich palette to winter's foggy freeze. In years past, the exposed rock would be jammed, sometimes to a great height, with the handiwork of upstream lumberjacks.

GATINEAU BALLOON FESTIVAL

There are few festivals around the world more visually spectacular than the Gatineau Hot Air Balloon Festival, which takes place in late summer over the city of Gatineau. Gatineau is a paper mill town and bedroom community to the east of Hull. Each year the city is host to "Le Festival de montgolfières de Gatineau". "Montgolfières", the proper French word for hot air balloons, is a word with tremendous historic importance for the French. In the 18th century, two French brothers, Joseph and Etienne Montgolfier (coincidentally paper makers), made the first manned ascent in a hot air balloon.

The festival is now into its second decade and it has grown to be one of the world's largest. The centrepieces of the event are the twice-daily mass balloon launches - one at sunrise and one before sundown. Over 100 hot air balloons of all shapes, sizes and colours (giant cows, eagles, Mounties, light bulbs, champagne bottles etc) take to the air and spread out across the horizon. Over 200,000 citizens from both sides of the river take part in the four days of festivities at Gatineau's Parc de la baie, but hundreds of thousands more across the city watch from whatever vantage point they can. Conditions look good for a launch - setting sun, unlimited visibility and light winds from the northwest about to carry the balloons over the river and the waiting boaters, much to the delight of all.

MILE OF HISTORY

The "Mile of History" passes in grand fashion from the National Gallery plaza to Rideau Street. Government planners, wishing to preserve Ottawa's history for all of Canada, coined the phrase and endeavoured to refurbish the length of Sussex Drive. It was already too late for the long line of elegant structures (right) on the west side of the street, which backed onto a twenty-foot escarpment. These were demolished to make way for the Connaught Building, as well as the wartime temporary buildings that occupied the present site of the new Embassy of the United States.

View north on Sussex Drive from George Street.

A long line of curio, book, fashion and antique shops takes advantage of both the sunlight and the crowds drawn to the attractions of the area.

(Above) This 1910 view looking north on Sussex Drive from George Street shows the Geological Survey Building and the second block of what we now call the "Mile of History".

One of the earliest structures on Sussex Drive still in existence, Notre Dame Basilica stands facing prominently up river. French Catholic raftsmen, back in 1848, who were about to risk their lives on the Chaudière slides, could easily see its twin 170-foot steeples and make a silent prayer to the golden statue of the Blessed Virgin and Child, which stands between the spires. Originally called a Cathedral, it has since been upgraded to Basilica status.

The National Gallery of Canada, located on the great open plaza at the corner of St. Patrick Street and Sussex Drive is, like the Museum of Civilization, one of the jewels in the crown of Canada's Capital. The crystal-like facets of the Moshe Safdie design reflect visual qualities to be found in the Parliament Buildings and in particular the Parliamentary Library. The Gallery houses an incredible permanent collection, featuring many diverse works, including those by Canada's Group of Seven. Several impressive touring exhibitions have also passed through its grand galleries in recent years, including Van Gogh, Degas, Renoir and Picasso.

Byward Market

The Byward Market has, since the beginning of Ottawa's history, been the heart, soul, purse and breadbasket of a thriving community. In Paul Alfred's richly textured painting (below) from 1928, we see that the delicious atmosphere of farm produce and chaotic traffic has been the hallmark of the Market for all time. The turreted mansard roof of the old Market Building on Byward Street is seen from York Street looking east. Lapointe's Fish Market, a long-standing Ottawa establishment, was obviously located here in the 1920s. The yellow brick building, seen here at the southeast corner of William and York, now caters to tourists as a seafood restaurant.

Paul Alfred / NATIONAL ARCHIVES OF CANADA / C-010536

Winter or summer, the market has always been a beehive of activity. In the cold winter light, captured by Franklin Brownell in the early 1900s (right), merchants and shoppers crowd the streets. Judging by the light, this is a view north to the often reconstituted main Market Building between Byward and William Streets. The air is crisp, with the snow squeaking underfoot. One can almost hear the snort and stomp of the draught horses, the jingle of sleigh bells and the shouts and laughter of a people who, like we today, enjoyed an outing to the marvellous Market.

Franklin Brownell / NATIONAL ARCHIVES OF CANADA / C-10533

(Left) When the Christmas season is close at hand, and the days are not too bitter, the crowds will return to the stalls for handmade wreaths, Christmas trees, fire wood and gifts. The warmth of coffee shops beckons and pubs are especially busy.

(Right) On a winter night, the strolling crowds are gone, but the Market sparkles with the enticing light of shop interiors.

The 20th century has produced more substantial change to the human condition than any other, but at the dawn of a new millennium, it's the old values that have resurfaced and remain strong. In these four images, we see an urban meeting place stand virtually unchanged for more than a century. In 1910 (top), though the first car has already made its debut, the horse is king. Looking across George Street, we peer not only down Byward Street, but also down the corridor of history. In only 10 years (middle), the technology change is spectacular. The horse has been deposed and the shiny new vehicles of the region's farmers give meaning to the new phrase - "truck farmers". In 1950 (bottom), the cars are bigger and more streamlined, but business goes on as usual. The exciting growth of the city parallels that of the country, which has hit its stride following WWII. The main market building has been replaced by a new and improved structure, offering covered yet open areas for the sale of produce.

These potted flowers will soon find new summer homes in gardens throughout the national Capital Region.

Today, the farmers' market has been reduced in size, since many of the farm products and the ways in which they were sold are no longer fashionable. Right up to the 1950s, shoppers could have a chicken, rabbit or goose slaughtered right in front of them. Animals for food were once part of the scene on York Street, but sensibilities being what they are, people nowadays prefer their meat pre-dressed at a butcher shop. Today the large open space is dedicated to cars and restaurant terraces. Desperate shoppers looking for the perfect spot still circle this block several times before they find one.

The gap of several generations melts away under a warm summer sun in the Market.

A double decker bus, with an open upper deck, gives riders the second best vantage point from which to experience the colour, smells and sounds of the Byward Market. The best, of course, would be to get out on foot and interact with the sellers under their colourful awnings; to squeeze the tomatoes, smell the flowers and taste the samples of fresh fruit and vegetables that are always offered.

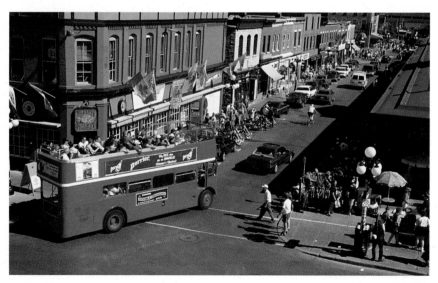

MACDONALD-CARTIER AIRPORT

The Ottawa International Airport today is a city unto itself. Fast food restaurants, bars, banking, bookstores and other businesses combine to take advantage of a captive clientele with anywhere from five minutes to five hours to spare. Ottawa, not being one of the big airline hubs, enjoys quick turnarounds and minimal delays for its passengers.

In 1927, Canada was in its sixtieth year and her airport, soon to become known as Lindberg Field in honour a special goodwill visit by Charles Lindbergh in that year, is a far cry from the modern facility pictured above.

The modern control tower for YOW (three-letter international code for Ottawa's airport) replaced the old one in the 1980s. It stands alone in the infield at the intersection of the two main runways.

In 1954, Canadians still looked upon airline travel as the sole privilege of the rich and famous. The passengers' waiting lounge at the Ottawa Airport in 1954 clearly shows us that few passengers were passing through its doors. A few chairs, a soft drink machine and a schedule rack make this lounge look more like a bus terminal in a deserted prairie town. Within a few years, things would change drastically.

CANADA DAY

134 years, and we've never stopped celebrating. Back in 1867, the year of Confederation, there was so much to celebrate. A new and great country was stepping on to the world stage. The fresh sandstone edifices of the Dominion's new government were almost complete and it was Queen Victoria's birthday. Thousands crowd the lawns of Parliament (inset upper left) to watch the military spectacle and share in one of our greatest moments. 131 years later, Canadians are still drawn by the thousands to where it all began. In 1867, July 1st (Dominion Day) was selected as our new National holiday and since then, Canada Day (as it became known in 1982) has become the greatest excuse of the summer for a party from coast to coast. Patriotic hot air balloons have the thousands below staring skyward as they drift lazily into the sunset.

(inset upper right) An RCMP officer poses for tourists' cameras in front of the Peace Tower of Canada's Parliament.

There are many wonderful vantage points around Entrance Bay from which to view the spectacular Canada Day fireworks display, but none are better that the lawns of Parliament Hill. Designed to be enjoyed from the Hill, the fireworks are a twenty-minute cannonade of colour, concussion and smoke.

ROYAL CANADIAN MOUNTED POLICE

Chaaaarge! In the thundering and heart-pounding finale to the world famous Musical Ride, red-serged Mounties demonstrate their equestrian skills and put the fear of God in the bad guys. During late spring and early summer, the Musical Ride offers up evening demonstrations of their spectacular precision horsemanship, free of charge to the citizens of Ottawa and tourists alike. And the citizens of Ottawa love a free show.

As the setting sun warms the buildings and grounds of the RCMP 'N' Division and Musical Ride stables near the eastern end of Rockcliffe Park, two members of "The Force", celebrating the 25th anniversary of women in the ranks, lower the flag at the setting of the sun.